EILEEN GRAY

Translated from the French by Anthony Rudolf

First published in Great Britain in 1998
by Thames and Hudson Ltd, London

British Library Cataloguing-in-Publication Data
A catalogue record for this book is available from the British Library

ISBN 0-500-01853-7

Printed in Italy

EILEEN GRAY

François Baudot

Thames and Hudson

eileen Gray, architect and decorative artist, remains one of the most attractive – and most mysterious – personalities in the galaxy which presided over the birth of contemporary design. A demanding and silent recluse, who found it impossible to assimilate herself into any group, she only narrowly escaped oblivion: her great shyness and the hermetism of her work never made her very approachable. Disconcerting in their day, the forms engendered by Eileen Gray have lost nothing of their novelty; this may explain why her designs, apart from the lacquer pieces, have remained in obscurity, familiar only to the initiated. Fortunately, however, this authentic creator, active until the end of her long life, has enabled a bridge to be built – just in time – between the pioneering epoch of modern artists and our own day. The high-tech style developed in New York and the minimalism which followed both owe much to the rigour, the laconism and the radicalism of artists like Eileen Gray – with one significant difference, namely that this aristocrat of design, more demanding of herself than of other people, never confused simplicity and poverty. An overview of her laborious and inspired work reveals one of the essential qualities of Eileen Gray: consistent with her discretion, each object, each project, each study of this *designer* in the modern sense of the word, affirms her supreme subtlety, a quality very rarely emphasized by the proponents of 'the beautiful in the useful'.

'One afternoon in the 1970s, in Paris, I went to see the architect and designer Eileen Gray who, at the age of ninety-three, found it quite natural to work fourteen hours a day. She lived in rue Bonaparte. In her living room she had hung a map of Patagonia, painted in gouache.
"I've always wanted to go there," I said.
"Me too," she said. "Go for me."
I went...Six months later I returned with the framework of a book which, this time, was published.'

Thus the prematurely deceased writer and adventurer, Bruce Chatwin, recounts the birth of his famous book *In Patagonia*, evoking one of the privileged relationships that Eileen Gray, a great armchair traveller towards the end of her life, succeeded in maintaining with a handful of singular people. Situated at 21 rue Bonaparte, the apartment remembered by Chatwin was the setting of Eileen Gray's life and work for about seventy years. She moved there in 1907, to the second floor of a fine eighteenth-century *hôtel*: four beautiful rooms in the shadow of Saint-Germain-des-Prés, then still an area with a village-like atmosphere. There she designed and sometimes realized the screens and doors, divans and sofas, chairs, tables, lamps and mirrors, and the majority of her architectural pieces – very few all in all – which demonstrate her particular genius. A genius exemplary of that period when determined members of what was for a long time called the 'fair sex' set about freeing themselves from the traditional roles which had weighed so heavily upon them.

b orn on 9 August 1878 in County Wexford, Ireland, into a distinguished but somewhat unconventional family, Eileen Gray was brought up at Brownswood, a large and uncomfortable country house. If she was to escape polite Victorian society, marriage was not the way she would go about it. At twenty, she had no trouble in obtaining her mother's permission to study painting in London. In Paris for the Universal Exhibition in 1900, Eileen Gray resolved to settle there, and did so two years later. She enrolled in the Ecole Colarossi in Montparnasse, then in the Académie Julian, where she rounded off an artistic training embarked upon at the Slade School in London. Thus was born a tranquil emancipation which she would never cease to affirm throughout her life. Tall, thin, soberly elegant and enhanced by a natural reserve many would take for coldness, Eileen Gray owed to her Irish origins a passion for nature as the source of life.

In 1904, she visited Tunisia, discovered the desert and the oases, experienced freedom, and rejected various suitors. But above all, her deeply practical spirit developed a passion for the decorative arts which were beginning to expand notably in Paris with the encouragement of the Société des Artistes Décorateurs, founded in 1901. Eileen Gray showed less interest in the baroque style and affectedness of Art Nouveau than in the Arts and Crafts movement born in England in the 1870s, as well as the Viennese Secession movement, which never dissociated purely decorative art from architecture and structural elements.

In 1905, at a loose end during a visit to London to see her ailing mother, Eileen Gray wandered into a lacquer-restoration studio. Its director, a Mr D. Charles, agreed to take her on as an apprentice. Coming from a young member of the Edwardian gentry, such initiative might seem surprising. But Eileen Gray was both obstinate and diligent, and thus returned to Paris with a certain amount of experience. In 1906, she befriended the Japanese lacquerer Sugawara, to whom the art of lacquer in France owes a great deal. Thanks to her desperately hard work and after many unsuccessful experiments – which sometimes required up to forty successive coats of lacquer – Eileen Gray, under the guidance of Sugawara, succeeded in executing several classic models in the hard, shiny material of the Japanese masters. But soon, through her personal research and experimentation, her output became more inventive – she would mix inlays of mother-of-pearl, silver or gold with lacquer. The purely abstract inspiration of this work remained free of all superfluous elements. Her collaboration with Sugawara was to last some forty years. During this time some highly skilled artisans, often trained by Eileen Gray, prepared the cabinet-work to her specifications ready for the application of precious lacquers, with their silken sheen. The virtuosity of Eileen Gray and Sugawara did not escape the notice of Jean Dunand, a sculptor who worked in copper. Dunand was searching for new ways of decorating the copperware pieces which he fashioned in the great Belgian tradition. As an admirer of Eileen Gray's work, he too asked Sugawara if he might receive instruction. In the 1920s, by then fully trained, Dunand became without question the most famous lacquer artist of the Art Deco generation. The young Eileen Gray, keen to explore new territory, pursued her infinitely varied œuvre in other directions.

the majority of designs from the first phase of Eileen Gray's career date from the very early years of the century, and as a result are contemporaneous with the first bars of Stravinsky, the infancy of Cubism and the dresses of Paul Poiret. Thus, almost unwittingly, Eileen Gray joined that small band of terrorists which brought the old world, not without some resistance, into a twentieth century that the Great War would prevent from flowering before its second decade. It was prophetic of her genius that Eileen Gray, like Picasso, Pierre Legrain, Giorgio de Chirico, Robert Delaunay and many others, was immediately understood by that prince of patrons, Jacques Doucet. A remote figure and a dandy who seemed only to be interested in himself, this couturier-Maecenas with the conventional manners of a *fin-de-siècle* high bourgeois fell for a red-lacquered screen with four panels, christened by Eileen Gray *Le Destin* in a moment of premonition. In addition to the abstract, sinuous patterns on its reverse, the screen is decorated with two youths, one of whom carries an old man in a shroud. Doucet bought *Le Destin* without hesitation, and it brought Eileen Gray public recognition for the first time. Oddly, it was *Le Destin* which was to refresh people's memories on 8 November 1972, the day of the sale at the Hôtel Drouot of the deceased couturier's chattels. Art Deco then was known only to a few connoisseurs, whereas 'retro' style was gathering momentum. The Doucet sale was the prelude to the immense interest which continues to this day in the 'antiques' of the twentieth century. The bidding for *Le Destin* reached the staggering figure of $36,000, more than enough for the newspapers to bring Eileen Gray out of voluntary exile by running articles about her throughout the world. Collectors entered the chase, and Yves Saint Laurent's interest completed the mythification of her image. Another prince of taste, the undisputed *arbiter elegantiae* of his day, Saint Laurent – half a century after Doucet – consolidated an admiration to which the old lady seemed completely indifferent: neither couture nor fashion had ever impressed her much.

Jacques Doucet, who kept the best of his collection of works of art in his celebrated 'studio' (alas no more) at Neuilly (to name but two, Le Douanier Rousseau's *The Snake Charmer*, which he bequeathed to the Louvre, and Picasso's *Les Demoiselles d'Avignon*, today the brightest jewel in the crown of the Museum of Modern Art in New York), commissioned several important pieces from the young artist. These were to enter his 'temple of modern art', which was described in *L'Illustration*, *Fémina* and the specialist art press. Today in the Saint Laurent collection, the Lotus table, lacquered in dark green with silk tassels at each corner weighted with four amber rings, is startling in its originality. But soon carpets were to capture Eileen Gray's imagination and contribute greatly to her fame, especially as they are so much easier to produce in number than lacquer pieces. With a childhood friend, Evelyn Wyld – another woman alone – Eileen Gray started a small factory in 1907. Wyld ran the factory, while Gray devoted her time to designing carpet patterns. During the 1920s, these became increasingly abstract, and close in style to the work of the most celebrated creator of textiles of that period, Bruno da Silva Bruhns. Woven with great care, these carpets sold better than Eileen Gray's other laboriously created works. The French Prime Minister of the day, Raymond Poincaré; the writer Maurice Martin du Gard; the Communist politician Maurice Thorez; the Vicomte Charles de Noailles; various artists and architects; various English and Dutch collectors – they all squabbled over these handwoven woollen floor-coverings.

during the dramatic interval of the Great War, Eileen Gray, ever loyal towards the country which had welcomed her, busied herself raising funds for the wounded. She worked as a supply nurse with some of her dearest friends, until she was forced to return to London where her mother was dying. When she returned to Paris in 1920, Eileen Gray found that everything had changed. Relations between art and society were governed by new rules. The time was ripe for Eileen Gray and women like her to spread their wings – drive a car, hang around with flying aces, wear Paul Poiret coats, cut your hair short…She began to resemble those boyish girls whom many women, not yet on the same footing as men, saw as superior beings. There was a small community of influential 'amazons' in Paris, centred on strong personalities like the American Natalie Clifford Barney who regularly hosted a literary salon at her apartment in the rue Jacob, or her fellow American Gertrude Stein who, in addition to possessing great talents as a writer, was assembling a major collection of modern art. These women, in their close communities, often fell out and then made up; they undoubtedly played their part in the evolution of manners and thinking. Though she always kept a slight distance, Eileen Gray associated with these groups, and her talent enjoyed a certain prestige among all of them. But it was to the charms of Marie-Louise Damien, a cabaret artist who used the name Damia, that she succumbed. A beautiful woman with a warm voice, one of the greatest singers of her kind, she inspired a fierce passion in the austere artist apparently so different from her. The one living under the spotlights, the other fleeing all notoriety, their intermittent relationship lasted until 1938, after which they never saw each other again, although both lived into their nineties in the same city, and cast the same curious, objective eye on everything that came their way.

The first part of Eileen Gray's career, which could be described, notwithstanding her own predilections, as fashionable, reached its acme in 1919 with her decoration of the apartment of the milliner Suzanne Talbot (Madame Mathieu-Lévy) in the rue de Lota. No longer a question of a few works of art, this was an ensemble whose accomplishment took four years, during which Eileen Gray elaborated – a good ten years ahead of her time – upon the rationalist concepts which René Herbst, Pierre Chareau, Le Corbusier and Robert Mallet-Stevens would propagate after 1929 with the founding of the 'Union des Artistes Modernes'. Eileen Gray herself was briefly a member. The extreme luxuriousness of her style was masked behind simplicity and unprecedented rigour in her designs for Suzanne Talbot: a black lacquer desk, a daybed with carved wooden feet, a dressing table of sycamore and ivory, a low armchair in red and yellow lacquer with arm-rests shaped like serpents (which now belongs to Yves Saint Laurent), and then the amazing

Pirogue sofa, like a dug-out canoe stuffed with matt gold cushions, whose lacquer resembled the pelt of an otter. No fewer than 450 brick panels were required for the hall walls, lacquered in black and texturized with eggshell, to give the appearance – striking in its modernity – of a lattice screen. The great wall panels in the salon were of dark lacquer, decorated with wave-like motifs of tarnished silver. Sugawara, with more work than he could handle, had to take on additional lacquerers. At floor level, the underlying influence on the design of the thick black carpets, punctuated with abstract motifs, was Cubism and its rhythms. These furnishings and fittings caused a sensation and were widely reproduced in newspaper photographs. Also for Suzanne Talbot, Eileen Gray designed the astonishing armchair known as Bibendum. Its seat and back were composed of three large white leather tubes, curved, stacked one upon another and mounted on a chrome-plated tubular support. A Futurist form, to say the least, evoking for us the 'inflatables' of the 1960s.

●

It seems unlikely that Eileen Gray much enjoyed playing interior decorator for worldly women whose whims contrasted sharply with her own preoccupations. The rue de Lota apartment, although it would not be repeated, at least allowed the innovator to put some of her schemes into practice. Conscious that henceforth she could only propagate her ideas in her own exhibition space, she acquired 217 rue du Faubourg Saint-Honoré, opposite the newly built concert hall, the Salle Pleyel. She had the long façade painted black, and the shop windows widened as much as possible and framed with white curtains. Most of the interior was lacquered in white. Finally, the height of incongruity, this boutique, run entirely by women, was christened with a mysterious man's name: Jean Désert. An anchorite in the burgeoning world of design, Eileen Gray was one of the very first to understand that in this century every break with the old order takes place via a metaphysic of the void. Don't prophets first have to preach in the desert? Inaugurated in 1922, the gallery proved that the decorative arts could be the business of women. In France, at that time, this was not self-evident. Although things were difficult at the start, an élite clientele purchased several rare pieces by Eileen Gray, but her productivity was hardly sufficient to yield much profit, and her female collaborators did not excel on the business side, something which Gray pretended not to notice. However, a visit to Jean Désert was described by the *Chicago Tribune* as a 'journey into the previously unseen'. Public esteem, as discreet as the woman who gave rise to it, was indeed there. It was primarily the Dutch avant-garde, in particular the De Stijl movement, which retained the most privileged links with Eileen Gray. A mutual influence encouraged the radicalization of her creative process. Her work became increasingly functionalist and abstract, close to that of Mondrian or Theo van Doesburg, two pillars of the De Stijl movement. In 1924, the magazine *Wendingen* (*Turning Point*) devoted an entire issue to her work. In it, Eileen Gray presented photographs of a wooden maquette (her first architectural study), and several of her new pieces of furniture, which henceforth adopt an aesthetic close to that of Gerritt Rietveld.

From now on her style would remain very far from the heavy-duty ornamentalism that so cluttered the exhibition 'Les Arts décoratifs' of 1925. Eileen Gray was not invited to participate, doubtless because her work was considered too extreme by the French jury. In 1926 she put her name to her first completed architectural project: a 'house for an engineer'. It was at this point in the course of her life that she met Jean Badovici, and it was with him that she conceived the 'house by the sea', also known as E.1027: E for Eileen; 10 for J (Jean's initial), the tenth letter of the alphabet; 2 for the second letter, B (his surname, Badovici); and 7 for G (Gray). This arduous project left a mark on the second stage of her life and gave rise to a new generation of artistic creations, her most prophetic works.

•

J ean Badovici, a handsome and impressive man, was born in Bucharest in 1893. Enamoured of the avant-garde and a theoretician of modern architecture, he was a friend of Le Corbusier and other champions of the new spirit in art. Having seen the quality of Eileen Gray's drawings and maquettes, he encouraged her to become an architect, despite her lack of formal training. At the age of 46, Eileen Gray was a novice, having only constructed wooden or cardboard maquettes. She began to teach herself the rudiments of architecture, all the more fired because Badovici had entrusted her with the elaboration of some plans for a 'little refuge' of his own on the Côte d'Azur. After a search for a building plot at the beginning of 1925, one was found at Roquebrune and, the following year, she embarked on one of the earliest buildings to exploit the modern vocabulary, using a covered terrace, *piloti* (concrete piers) and horizontal openings. With an elliptical stairway giving access to the basement and the terrace roof, and the open layout of the main room achieved by self-supporting walls, House E.1027 is an unblemished model of rationality. Inner and outer spaces interpenetrate with a remarkable fluidity which extends quite naturally into the steeply sloping garden. The fittings inside the house merge beautifully with the whole. Henceforth Eileen Gray's furniture and accessories became an intimate complement to their architectural settings. These elements of construction harmonize functionalism and a sophistication rarely attained in contemporary furniture. In addition to the Centimètre carpet which, against a black background, reproduces the graduations of the metric system, Eileen Gray created some of her finest pieces for Roquebrune. These include the Bedside table E.1027 in chrome-plated tubing whose top can be adjusted to the desired height, not to mention the superb Transat chair in lacquered wood, chrome-plated tubing and leather. Tables, chairs, cupboards and mirrors each embody a flexibility almost reminiscent of camp-site furniture: the house and its contents could be rearranged at will.

there was a humour, an irony, an individuality, a sophistication quite unique to this Anglo-Irishwoman, whose watchwords were freedom, comfort, aestheticism and individuality. In 1930, a year after the Wall Street Crash, her business affairs were showing no improvement and she closed Jean Désert. The adventure had lasted nearly ten years, surely a record for such an experiment in the avant-garde. The architect-designer did not allow herself to be dismayed by this setback; although it had cost her dear in worry and money, Jean Désert had brought her some satisfaction too. None of these astonishing prototypes ever went into production as had been intended. It was not until the end of the 1970s that Zeev Aram embarked, in London, on a limited reproduction of her designs. But Eileen Gray never knew of the success of her furniture. Around the same time, with extraordinary perseverance, the stylist Andrée Putman applied herself to the task of reproducing the series of Transats, Satellite mirrors and storage units which today make that boyish girl of the roaring twenties our exact contemporary, forever young. While so many architects, her macho contemporaries, were steeped in extremist theories, Eileen Gray remained a woman and a well-to-do amateur – quite enough to inflict serious damage upon her credibility.

Bibliography

Peter Adam, *Eileen Gray, Architect, Designer: A Biography*, Abrams and Thames and Hudson, New York and London, 1987.

Stewart Johnson, *Eileen Gray, Designer, 1876–1976*, Debrett in association with the Victoria and Albert Museum, catalogue of the eponymous exhibition, London, 1979.

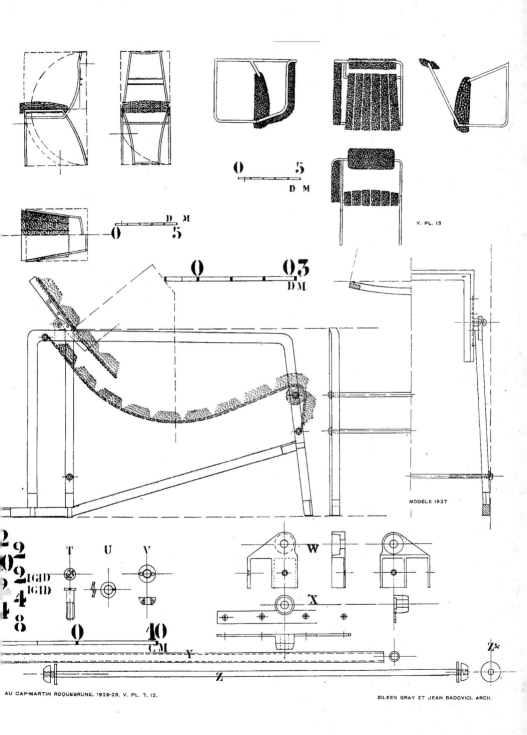

V. PL. 13

MODÈLE 1927

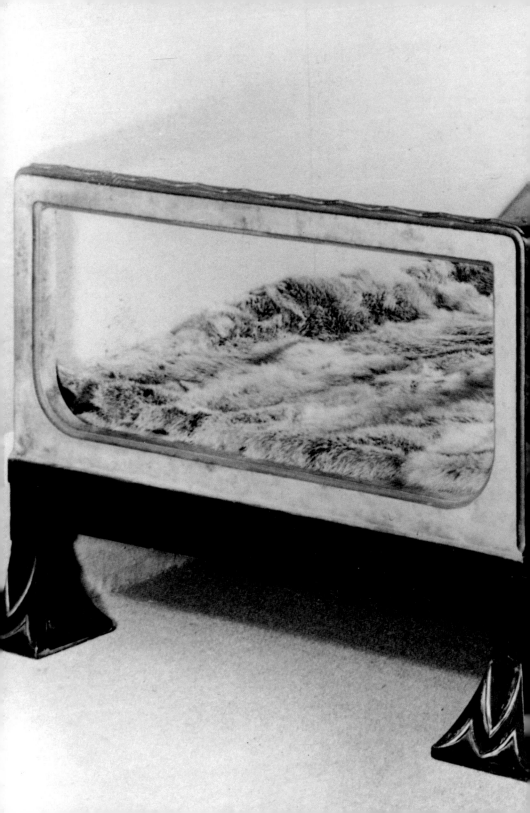

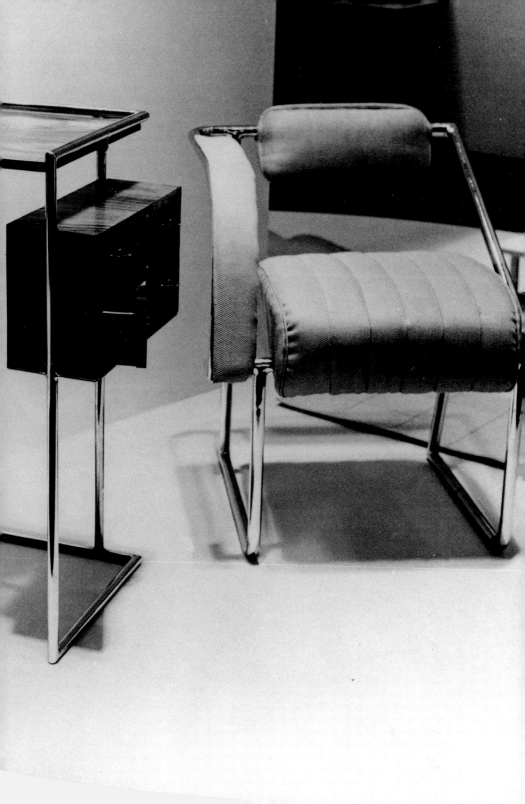

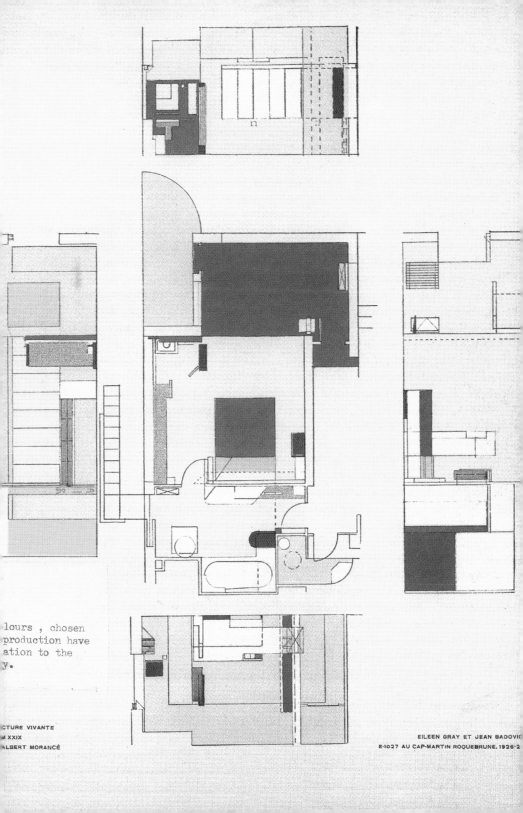

CTURE VIVANTE
M XXIX
ALBERT MORANCÉ

EILEEN GRAY ET JEAN BADOVIC
E-1027 AU CAP-MARTIN ROQUEBRUNE, 1926-2

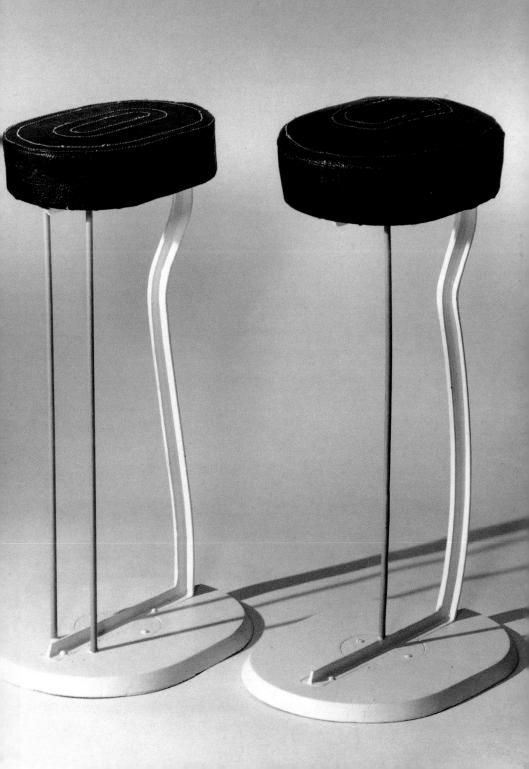

Chronology

1878	9 August, birth of Eileen Gray in Ireland in the family home, Brownswood (County Wexford).
1900	She discovers Paris on a visit for the Universal Exhibition.
1901	Eileen Gray attends the Slade School of Fine Arts, part of the University of London, in Bloomsbury.
1902	She moves to Paris and enrols at a painting school, the Ecole Colarossi, on the rue de la Grande Chaumière in Montparnasse, later moving to the Académie Julian, on the rue de Dragon.
1903	First Salon d'Automne in the basement of the Petit Palais. Eileen Gray discovers the work of Bonnard, Gauguin, Seurat and Van Gogh, among others.
1904–5	On a visit to Tunisia, she is captivated by the desert. While walking in Dean Street in London, Eileen Gray happens upon a lacquer-restoration studio, which she joins to learn this Japanese technique. Returning to Paris at the end of 1906 she befriends the lacquer master, Sugawara, under whose auspices she completes her training. They will work together for many years, Sugawara executing her designs.
1907	Eileen Gray decides to settle in Paris. She acquires an apartment at 21 rue Bonaparte, near the square of Saint-Germain-des-Prés, where she will live and work for nearly seventy years.
1908	Eileen Gray meets Jean Dunand who learns the technique of lacquer under Sugawara's tutelage. Dunand will become the technique's most brilliant exponent during the 1920s.
1909	Eileen Gray discovers the Ballets-Russes and the designs of Léon Bakst. She buys her first car, a Chenard Walker.
1911	The Cubists show their work at the Salon des Indépendants: an aesthetic revolution is underway.
1912	Eileen Gray's lacquer panels are beginning to be well known. Her first transatlantic crossing takes her to New York, which inspires her greatly.
1913	Eileen Gray is invited to exhibit some of her work at the VIII Salon des Artistes Décorateurs. Fashionable society discovers her, particularly the couturier Jacques Doucet and the celebrated and influential hostess Elisabeth de Gramont, Duchess of Clermont-Tonnerre, who writes an article about her. Jacques Doucet sees a screen with four panels, *Le Destin*, in Eileen Gray's studio and buys it. When Doucet's possessions were auctioned by Drouot in Paris in 1972, *Le Destin* fetched a record price of $36,000, generating renewed interest in its creator.
1914–20	During 1914, Eileen Gray works as a supply nurse in a makeshift hospital on the Champs-Elysées for soldiers wounded in the war. Commissioned by Jacques Doucet to make works for his collection, Eileen Gray produces some of her most beautiful lacquer pieces, including the Lotus table, two low tables and a red and blue lacquer wardrobe which 'opened up like a *boutique*'.
1918	Le Corbusier and Amédée Ozenfant publish their Purist manifesto *Après le Cubisme* (*After Cubism*).
1919	Eileen Gray embarks on the epoch-making decoration of an apartment for Madame Mathieu-Lévy, the milliner Suzanne Talbot, for whom she creates the famous Pirogue sofa.

Chest of drawers, 1919–22; zebra wood scorched in the Japanese manner, with ivory handles and black lacquer top. Private collection. Photo © Cabinet d'expertises Camard, Paris.

1922	Opening at 217 rue du Faubourg Saint-Honoré of Jean Désert, Eileen Gray's gallery in which she displayed her furniture, carpets and lights. On 4 July, the *Chicago Tribune* devotes a eulogistic article to her, entitled 'Furniture in Bizarre Forms and Styles'.
1923	At the XIV Salon des Artistes Décorateurs in Paris Eileen Gray displays an entire room, the Bedroom-boudoir for Monte Carlo, which comes to the attention of De Stijl, the influential Dutch avant-garde movement.
1924	The Dutch magazine *Wendingen* (*Turning Point*), which has close links with De Stijl, devotes a special issue to Eileen Gray.
1925	The pavilions at the exhibition 'Les Arts décoratifs' display thousands of works by architects and decorative artists from around the globe. No one thinks to invite Gray to participate in this magnificent display, which gave its name to the style now known as Art Deco.
1926	At the prompting of her friend Jean Badovici, a theoretician of modern architecture closely linked to Le Corbusier, Eileen Gray embarks on a career as an architect, without any previous training.
1928	Eileen Gray puts the finishing touches to her most comprehensive achievement, House E.1027 at Roquebrune-Cap-Martin on the Côte d'Azur, conceiving its architecture, its revolutionary interior design, and its furniture, some of which uses chrome-plated tubing for the first time.
1929	The writer and art dealer Henri-Pierre Roché (future author of the autobiographical novel *Jules and Jim*, which inspired Truffaut's famous film) introduces Eileen Gray to the Maharajah of Indore, whose kingdom is about 350 miles from Bombay. For his ultra-modern palace, built in four years by Eckhart Muthesius, she provides two Transat chairs in lacquered wood, chrome-plated tubing and leather.
1930	The Depression forces Eileen Gray to close Jean Désert and disperse its stock. During the 1930s, she devotes her energies to planning a home at Castellar, near Menton. For the rest of her life (dividing her time between Castellar and rue Bonaparte) she devotes herself to town-planning projects, architecture and furniture prototypes, most of which were never executed.
1975	Eileen Gray grants permission to Zeev Aram Design, London to reproduce her designs.
1976	Eileen Gray dies at home in Paris on 31 October. Her ashes are deposited in the cemetery of Père Lachaise.
1979	The Victoria and Albert Museum in London and the Scottish Arts Council Gallery in Edinburgh present major retrospectives of Eileen Gray's work.
1980	In New York, the Museum of Modern Art organizes an exhibition of Eileen Gray's work, and the Rosa Elman Gallery mounts an exhibition of her carpet designs.
1980s–90s	At the prompting of its founder, the stylist Andrée Putman, the company Ecart International reproduces five of Eileen Gray's pieces. By now, she is considered to be one of the pioneers of international design.
1997	The Deutsches Architektur-Museum and the Museum für Kunsthandwerk in Frankfurt mount a major retrospective exhibition, entitled 'Eileen Gray: An Architecture for All Senses'.

Small lacquer panel, made *c.* 1913, depicting a woman in a Japanese landscape, in a black lacquer frame with a rose. The frame is probably the work of Sugawara. Collection Vallois. Photo © Galerie Vallois, Paris.

Eileen Gray

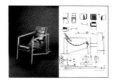

Transat (*transatlantique*) chair, 1925–6, for House E.1027; wood, chrome-plated tubing, leather-upholstered seat. Private collection. Photo © Galerie Doria, Paris. **Preparatory sketches** for dining room chair (top left), Nonconformist armchair (top right) and Transat chair. Private collection. Photo © Eileen Gray Archive, London.

Lampstand, 1923; lacquer, with a vellum lampshade. Collection Vallois. Photo © Galerie Vallois, Paris. Bench, 1920–2; macassar ebony with amaranth and lemontree inlay and leather pad. Collection Vallois. Photo © Galerie Vallois, Paris.

Le Destin, 1913; lacquer screen with four panels. For the couturier Jacques Doucet. Private collection. **Pirogue sofa**, 1919–20; lacquer resembling an otter's pelt. For the apartment of the milliner Suzanne Talbot in the rue de Lota, Paris. Private collection. Photo © Eileen Gray Archive, London.

Dining room table (detail), for House E.1027, 1926–9; chrome-plated tubing with cork to eliminate the noise of dishes. Private collection. Photo © Galerie Doria, Paris. **Table E.1027** (detail), 1926–9; chrome-plated tubing, various tops. Private collection. Photo © Galerie Doria, Paris.

Eileen Gray's bedroom, c. 1930, in her rue Bonaparte apartment, where she lived until her death in 1976. Photo © Eileen Gray Archive, London.

Dressing table, 1919–22; oak and sycamore stained black, with glass top. Private collection. Photo © Eileen Gray Archive, London. **Detail of pivoting drawer** of same dressing table showing carved ivory handle. Photo © Eileen Gray Archive, London.

Detail of leg of *guéridon* showing African-inspired leg design in silver lacquer.
Photo © Documentation Maria de Beyrie, Paris.
Two-tier round table (*guéridon*) with a *bilboquet* (cup and ball) design, before
1917; lacquer with red lacquer inlay. For Jacques Doucet. Private collection.
Photo © Documentation Maria de Beyrie, Paris.

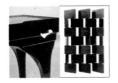

Desk; black lacquer with carved ivory handles. For the Monte Carlo Bedroom-
boudoir exhibited at the XIV Salon des Artistes Décorateurs in Paris in 1923.
Collection Vallois. Photo © Galerie Vallois, Paris.
Block screen, 1922–5; black lacquer panels with connecting metal rods. Private
collection. Photo © Eileen Gray Archive, London.

The Paris studio of Jacques Doucet, on the rue Saint-James, with Eileen Gray's
Bilboquet table, a sofa by Marcel Couard, and Le Douanier Rousseau's *The
Snake Charmer*. The door, in crystal, is by René Lalique. Photo published on
3 May 1930 in *L'Illustration*. Photo © *L'Illustration*/Sygma, Paris.

Egyptian-inspired daybed, 1919–22; carved wood, grey, blue and black
lacquer. For Suzanne Talbot's rue de Lota apartment; here shown arranged as
a sofa. Collection Vallois. Photo © Galerie Vallois, Paris.

Lotus table for Jacques Doucet, *c.* 1913; dark green lacquer, with silk tassels
weighted with amber rings added at Doucet's suggestion. Private collection.
Photo © Documentation Maria de Beyrie, Paris.

Jacques Doucet's studio, showing Eileen Gray's Lotus table in a photograph
published on 3 May 1930 in *L'Illustration*. Photo © *L'Illustration*/Sygma, Paris.

Design for the Marine carpet for House E.1027, *c.* 1925. Private collection.
Photo © Eileen Gray Archive, London.
House E.1027 at Roquebrune-Cap-Martin from the sea, 1926–9. The first
realized house design by Eileen Gray. Photo © Eileen Gray Archive, London.

Lamp, 1919–25; carved ebony. Collection Vallois. Photo © Galerie Vallois, Paris. **Head of a woman**, carved by Sugawara; black and chocolate-coloured lacquer. Private collection. Photo © Cabinet d'expertises Camard, Paris.

Screen, 1922–5; lacquered wood in relief and silver leaf. Victoria and Albert Museum, London. Photo © Eileen Gray Archive, London.

Table (detail), c. 1913; red and black lacquer. For Jacques Doucet. Collection Vallois. Photo © Galerie Vallois, Paris.
The same table, in a photograph published on 3 May 1930 in *L'Illustration*, in the hall of Jacques Doucet's studio. Photo © *L'Illustration*/Sygma, Paris.

Table E.1027, 1926–9; chrome-plated tubing, various tops. One of Eileen Gray's most famous designs, it can be raised and lowered to bring the tray to the desired height. Private collection. Photo © Eileen Gray Archive, London. **Eileen Gray** in c. 1913. Photo © Eileen Gray Archive, London.

Daybed, 1919–22; carved wood, orange and bright chestnut lacquer, with silver inlay. Private collection. Photo © Eileen Gray Archive, London.

Standard lamp, 1919–25; lacquer. Collection Vallois. Photo © Galerie Vallois, Paris.
Detail of the lamp's stand, whose form is redolent of the Cubists. Photo © Galerie Vallois, Paris.

Dressing table, 1919–25; chrome-plated tubing and rosewood, with pivoting drawers. Private collection. **Nonconformist armchair**, 1926–8; continuous chrome-plated tubing and beige canvas. One arm was eliminated to allow freedom of movement. Private collection. Photo © Eileen Gray Archive, London.